RESOLUTION OF GERMAN BUNDESTAG

Of 02/06/2016 CONCERNING 1915 EVENTS

Author

Melih AKKURT, Attorney

Publisher

Cosmo Publishing

Cosmo
Publishing
Company

ISBN: 9781795695916

Preface

As protection of human rights is of capital importance in order to secure the humanitarian values and rights which are inviolable and untransferable, it necessitates not using the human rights for political, strategic and diplomatic purposes.

The only way to protect and secure human rights is through establishment of the rule of law over everything and everybody. Rule of law is one of the musts of protection of human rights and development of democracy.

Unfortunately, we observe that the Western Democracies shape the law according to their objectives and within the frame of their theories, rules and arguments at the present time.

The genocide resolution of German Federal Parliament and the decision given by the German Federal Constitutional Court with regard to this resolution exemplifies that law is politicised.

Especially the decision of Constitutional Court proves that the days when there were judges in Berlin came to an end and it brings to mind the days when Soghomon Tehlirian, who assassinated Talat Pascha in Berlin, on 15.03.1921 was "acquitted" after "being judged" for one day.

Our study involves the genocide resolution of German Federal Parliament dated 02.06.2016 and legal assessment of the decision accepted unanimously by German Federal Constitutional Court in the lawsuit brought against the said resolution.

It is possible to write thousands of pages about the matter but as the assessments were made only from legal point of view historic data, information and documents which would reveal the justness of Turkish arguments are not included.

I sincerely wish our study would provide an insight to international community and all legists.

Atty. Melih AKKURT

Resolution of German Bundestag of 02.06.2016 Concerning 1915 Events and Assessment of Verdict Given by German Federal Constitutional Court With Respect To Aforementioned Resolution

1. Introduction

Following the adoption of the allegation of genocide carried out by Turks against Armenians by national and supra-national or regional parliaments of Nederland, Poland, Slovakia, Russia, Argentina, Uruguay, France, Belgium, Southern Cyprus, USA and EU, it is also adopted by German Bundestag on 02.06.2016, on the 101st anniversary of the events in 1915 and on approximately fiftieth anniversary of Turkey's application to European Community for full membership.

When the issue is probed specific to Germany, a petition titled *"It is time to condemn the genocide"* was submitted to German Bundestag in April 2000. A year later, this petition was conveyed to German Foreign Ministry with an inscription stating *"The wounds should be healed instead of reopening them"* by the petition committee of parliament. Petition Committee pointed out in their press release on 10 October 2001 that the German Foreign Affairs attended to this matter in June 2001 and stated that the common history of Armenians and Turks is being addressed unofficially by non-governmental organizations in Turkey. Committee dropped the subject thus and so.

German Foreign Ministry's reply to another parliamentary question concerning the matter in September 2002 was: *"Bringing the past into the present is primarily a subject between the related countries, Armenia and Turkey… Federal Government considers all initiatives serving to address the sad events between the years of 1915 and 1917 appropriate. The results of these researches should be commented on by historians and legists. But attention should be paid to heal the wounds instead of reopen them."*

Same reply was given to parliamentary question of Erwin Marschewski, parliamentarian of Christian Union Parties on 29 December 2004 regarding the opinion of the Government of Federal Germany regarding the demand by Armenians the genocide to be recognized and whether Germany would bring this matter into question within the frame of negotiations between Turkey and EU.

In spite of all these developments and even if no new evidences came in view, adoption of the resolution by German Parliament on 02.06.2016 and support given to this resolution by German Government proves that the resolution of German legislative and executive organ is far from being objective.

It is necessary to assess the parliament's resolution in terms of politics, economics and strategy and the public opinion should be told that this resolution, especially from legal point of view, is wrong.

2. Resolution of Parliament and Its Legal Status

The following points were made by the resolution of German Bundestag dated 02.06.2016: The Ottoman Empire carried out a genocide against some Christian communities, Armenians, Assyrian and Chaldean Christians being in the first place, German Empire, the main military ally of Ottoman Empire participated in this genocide, therefore it is necessary for Germany to assist Turkey and Armenians to be drawn together due to its historic responsibility, this is important to provide stability in Caucasus and hence it bears a special responsibility within the frame of EU neighbourhood policy.

Within the frame of the points in resolution Federal Parliament requested from the Federal Government and commissioned it to encourage Turks to confront the genocide, continue to make an effort to provide the historic crime to be forgiven between Turks and Armenians by mutually facing the past, support scientific and cultural activities and activities of civil society serving communication, rapprochement and confrontation and continue to encourage within the frame of resources provided by the budget, actively supporting nongovernmental organizations showing an effort to achieve these purposes and their confrontation, encourage representatives of government to continue the normalization process of Turkish-Armenian relationships and finally make an effort to establish a committee in order to explore the history scientifically as undersigned in 2009, reinitialize diplomatic relations and provide approval of Zurich Protocols anticipating the opening of the common border by Turkish and Armenian governments.

Aforementioned points and assessments were not made by law but by an act of parliament.

It is stated in doctrine that the parliamentary resolution should be subject to judicial control as below;

- *" Constitutional complaint is a way stipulated against a violation of a fundamental right by "public power". The concept of "public power" mentioned here involves all government organs, namely legislative, executive and judicial organs. Therefore the subject of a constitutional complaint might be about the laws legislated by the Legislative organ or other transactions as well as administrative transactions or court decisions."*[1],

---

[1] Prof. Dr. Rudolf Mellinghof, Federal Almanya Cumhuriyetinde Anayasa Şikayeti (Constitutional Complaint in Federal Republic of Germany), Constitutional Court Publications, Ankara, 2009, p. 36

- " It is stated in Article 1/I of the Constitution of Federal Germany that human dignity is inviolable and it is the duty of state power to respect and protect it. In Paragraph 3 of the same article the provision that fundamental rights bind legislative, executive and judicial organs is stated. Pursuant thereto legislative, executive and judicial organs should be understood from the term "public power" mentioned in Article 93 of Constitution and in Article 90 of Constitutional Court Law (AYMK)." [2],

- " Public power paragraph in Article 93 (1) (4a) regulates that constitutional complaint applications can be made all kinds of governmental acts containing adjudications, administrative decisions and legislative acts."[3]

3. Assessment of Resolution in terms of Equality

The genocide[4] carried out by Armenians in Ottoman State and Hocalı Massacre against Azerbaijani Turks are not mentioned in Parliament's resolution and even though it refers to Zurich Protocol, there is no decretive regarding non-execution of 4 different ante-dated (1993) resolutions of General Assembly of United Nations is a mistake and thus the stability in Caucasus and Azerbaijan and Georgia located

---

http://www.anayasa.gov.tr/files/pdf/anayasa_yargisi/rudolfmellinghof.pdf (Access: 18.08.2016)

[2] Ece Göztepe, Anayasa Şikayeti (Constitutional Complaint), AnkaraUniversity Faculty of Law Publications No: 530, Ankara, 1998, p. 42

[3] Dieter Dörr, Die Verfassungsbeschverde in der Prozesspraxis, München, Carl Heymanns Verlag KG, 1990, s.23, a.g.e., p.195, quoted by Donald P. Kommers and Russell A. Miller, The Constitutional Jurisprudence of the Federal Republic of Germany, p.12

[4] Tverdohlebon, Gördüklerim Yaşadıklarım, Ed. Ahmet Tetik, Genel Kurmay Askeri Tarih ve Stratejik Etüt Başkanlığı Yayınları, Ankara, 2007. The word "genocide" has not been included in the study terminologically; since the term "genocide" was not invented at the time of the case. It is understood that the massacres were accepted as genocide.

in Caucasus are disregarded and only Armenia is taken into consideration.

It is stated in UN Security Council's first resolution dated 30 April 1993 no. 822 [5]that the territorial integrities and sovereignties of the states in the region should be respected, international borders could not be changed by force and Armenian troops should retreat from Kalbajar and other regions they occupied in Nagorno-Karabakh.

UN Security Council made reference to its resolution no. 822 in its second resolution dated 29 July 1993 no. 853[6] and issued a call for Armenian troops to retreat from Agdam and other regions they occupied in Nagorno-Karabakh.

While UN Security Council invites the parties to directly negotiate in its resolution dated 14 October 1993 no. 874[7], reference made to resolution to previous resolutions of UN Security Council in its resolution dated 12 November 1993 no. 884[8] and occupation of Azerbaijan territories by Armenians is condemned and it is requested from Armenia to end supporting Armenians living in Nagorno-Karabakh.

Furthermore considering the influence of Armenia on Armenians in Nagorno-Karabakh it is demanded from Armenia to carry the UN Security Council's resolutions into effect.

---

[5] For full text of resolution go to UN Official Web Page,
http://www.un.org/ga/search/view_doc.asp?symbol=S/RES/822(1993), (Access Date: 30.07.2016).
[6] For full text of resolution go to UN Official Web Page,
http://www.un.org/ga/search/view_doc.asp?symbol=S/RES/853(1993), (Access Date: 30.07.2016).
[7] For full text of resolution go to UN Official Web Page,
http://www.un.org/ga/search/view_doc.asp?symbol=S/RES/874(1993), (Access Date: 30.07.2016).
[8] For full text of resolution go to UN Official Web Page,
http://www.un.org/ga/search/view_doc.asp?symbol=S/RES/884(1993), (Access Tarihi: 30.07.2016).

As it is seen there is no uncertainty from the viewpoint of international community that the territories of Nagorno-Karabakh belong to Azerbaijan and these territories are occupied by Armenians but nevertheless, Germany's ignorance of conveyed issues is clearly against the principle of equality.

Resolution is only for the benefit of Christians and no mention is made about any Muslim faced with Armenian atrocity. To tell the truth, the resolution even didn't include Christian Georgians except Armenians. As it is known Armenia fought with Georgia in 1918. Therefore it is not realistic trying to introduce Armenians as a part of Crusader Army who fought against Muslim Turks in the resolution and it is also against equality due to ignorance of Georgians.

In article 11 of Armenian Declaration of Independence dated 23 August 1990 the following provision is stated with respect to borders; *"The Republic of Armenia stands in support of the task of achieving international recognition of the 1915 genocide in Ottoman Turkey and Western Armenia[9]."* At the beginning of Armenian Constitution it is also stated that; *"The Armenian People, recognize it as a basis the fundamental principles of the Armenian statehood and national aspirations engraved in the Declaration of Independence of Armenia."*[10] [11]

---

[9] The Republic of Armenia Stands in Support of the Task of Achieving İnternational Recognition of the 1915 Genocide in Ottoman Turkey and Western Armenia."
Armenian Declaration of Independence, 11,
http://www.gov.am/en/independence/2010-08-01.

[10] *"The Armenian People, recognizing as a basis the fundamental principles of the Armenian statehood and national aspirations engraved in the Declaration of İndependence of Armenia, having fulfilled the sacred message of its freedom loving ancestors for the restoration of the sovereign state, committed to the strengthening and prosperity of the fatherland, to ensure the freedom, general well-being and civic harmony of future generations, declaring their faithfulness to universal values, hereby adopts the Constitution of the Republic of Armenia"*,
http://www.parliament. am/parliament.php?id=constitutionvelang=eng2010-08-01.

[11] Regarding dissolution of USSR, establishment of Commonwealth of Independent States and status of new republics, it is stated in Article 5 of Minsk Treaty dated 8 December 1991 that member countries *"...recognize each other's integrities of state and inviolableness of existing borders..."* This principle is repeated in Alma Ata Declaration

Article 11 of the declaration which the Armenian Constitution is based on draws a border as a constitutional duty but not as a historic memory or a wish as will be pointed out below. The conclusion of this statement is the phrase of "West Armenia" implies Eastern Anatolia. Thus Armenia alleges that some of the Turkish territories belongs to Armenia and indirectly stakes a claim on these territories. In other words, they indirectly disregard the border between two countries.

The region[12] shown as "West Armenia" in historic atlases of Armenia and on website of Armenian Foreign Ministry involves a large part of Eastern and South Eastern Regions and some part of Eastern Black Sea Region of Turkey.

---

dated 21 December 1991 and signed by Armenia. Being one of the first founding documents of Commonwealth of Independent States established during the dissolution of Soviet Union, it is stated in Article 5 of Minsk Treaty that member countries ""...*recognize each other's integrities of state and inviolableness of existing borders...*". Principle of respect to integrity of state and inviolability of existing borders is repeated in Alma Ata Declaration dated 21 December 1991 and signed by Armenia.

But it is recorded in first protocol that the existing border between two countries is mutually recognized. Constitutional resolution expresses that this recognition is related with execution of normal transactions at passage points. That is, the border is recognized for execution of passing transactions. It is a factual recognition and doesn't mean that Turkey's territorial integrity is recognized. In other words Armenia could allege that they have historic rights and demand some territories from Turkey at a time they see convenient.

Lütem, Ömer Ergin, 2010" *Protokollerde Sıfır Noktasına Dönüş (Returning to Zero Point in Protocols)"*,

[12] Armenia through out the history, http://www. Armenica.org; Access: 5 June 2014, Historical Map of Armenia,
http://www.armeniaforeignministry.com, Access: 5 June 2014

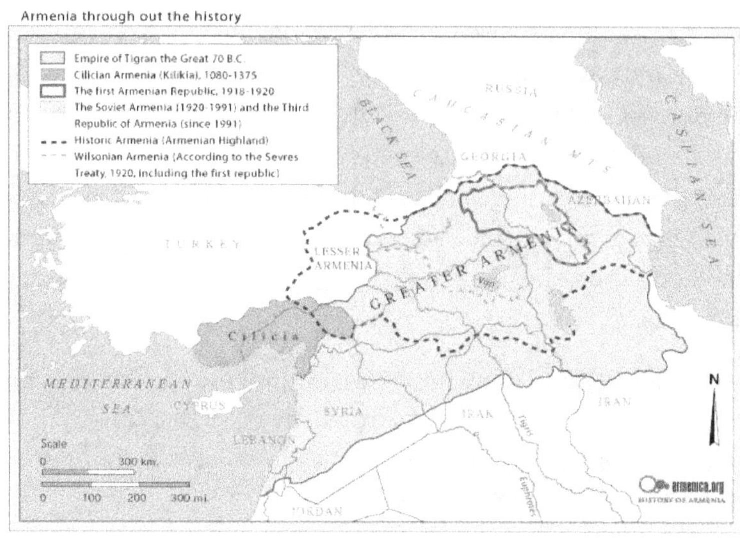

The region Armenia calls as West Armenia and shows in its territory involves 19 provinces of the Republic of Turkey at the present time: These provinces are below:

1. Erzurum	11. Siirt
2. Erzincan	12. Diyarbakır
3. Ağrı	13. Mardin
4. Van	14. Elazığ
5. Hakkari	15. Malatya
6. Bitlis	16. Bingöl
7. Muş	17. Sivas
8. Şırnak	18. Amasya
9. Van	19. Tokat
10. Batman	20. Some parts of Giresun

In the beginning of Armenian Constitution it is stated that *"Armenian people recognize the Armenian Declaration of Independence as fundamental principles of Armenian state and their national spirit."* In article 6 there is the prevision of; *"International agreements not complying with Armenian Constitution shall not be approved."* Article 13 states that *"The emblem of the Republic of Armenia consists Mount Ararat[13], Noah's Ark and emblems of 4 Armenian kingdoms."*

Armenian Parliament adopted a termination resolution on 6 December 1989 and declared that they don't accept the Turkey-Armenia border which was determined by the Treaty of Moscow on 16 March 1921.

Armenia's indicating some part of the territory of the Republic of Turkey as its territory and incorporating this allegation into its constitution is a clear violation of the provision stated in Section I, Article 2, Paragraph 4 under the title of Objectives and Principles of the Charter of the United Nations which expresses; *"All countries shall avoid both resorting to threat of use of force or use of force against the territorial integrity or politic independence of another country or in any way which doesn't comply with the objectives of the United Nations."*

Even though the aforementioned constitutional regulations break down the stability in Caucasus, German Bundestag did not take any notice of and ignore them and this a clear defiance of equality.

Resolution of Parliament and valuing Armenian community above is also a clear racial discrimination.

In fact while mentioning Germany's violation of **articles 2, 4 and 6 of International Convention on the Elimination of**

---

[13] Mount Ararat and province of Ağrı are within the borders of Republic of Turkey

All Forms of Racial Discrimination, United Nations Committee on the Elimination of Racial Discrimination stated following justifications in its **Communication No: 48/2010, CERD/C/82/D/48/2010**; *"The Committee considers that the above statements contain ideas of racial superiority, denying respect as human beings and depicting generalized negative characteristics of the Turkish population, as well as incitement to racial discrimination in order to deny them access to social welfare and speaking about a general prohibition of immigration influx except for highly qualified individuals, within the meaning of article 4 of the Convention."* The communication continues by expressing;" The *Committee recommends that the State party review its policy and procedures concerning prosecution in cases of alleged racial discrimination consisting of dissemination of ideas of superiority over other ethnic groups based on article 4 (a) of the Convention and of incitement to discrimination on such grounds, in the light of its obligations under article 4 of the Convention. The State party is also requested to give wide publicity to the Committee's Opinion, including among prosecutors and judicial bodies,"* and determines efficient methods to fight against racial discrimination.[14]

4. Contrariety of Resolution to Ante-Dated Resolutions

A petition titled *"It is time to condemn the genocide"* was submitted to German Bundestag in April 2000. A year later, this petition was conveyed to German Foreign Ministry with an inscription stating *"The wounds should be healed instead of reopening them"* by the petition committee of parliament. Petition Committee pointed out in their press release on 10 October 2001 that the German Foreign Affairs attended to this matter in June 2001 and stated that the common history of

---

[14] For resolution visit. http://www2.ohchr.org/English/bodies/cerd/docs/CERD-C-82-D-48-2010-English.pdf Access: 17.08.2016

Armenians and Turks is being addressed unofficially by non-governmental organizations in Turkey.[15] Committee dropped the subject thus and so[16]. German Foreign Ministry replied another parliament question in the matter in September 2002 as follows: *"Bringing the past into the present is primarily a subject between the related countries, Armenia and Turkey... Federal Government considers all initiatives serving to address the sad events between the years of 1915 and 1917 appropriate. The results of these researches should be commented on by historians and legists. But attention should be paid to heal the wounds instead of reopen them."[17]*

Same reply was given to parliamentary question of Erwin Marschewski, parliamentarian of Christian Union Parties on 29 December 2004 regarding the opinion of the Government of Federal Germany regarding the demand by Armenians the genocide to be recognized and whether Germany would bring this matter into question within the frame of negotiations between Turkey and EU. [18]

In spite of all these developments and even if no new evidences came in view, adoption of the resolution by German Parliament on 02.06.2016 and support given to this resolution by German Government proves that the resolution of German

---

[15] Anette Schaefgen, Der Vörlkmord an den Armeniern in der deutschen Politik nach 1949 (Armenian Genocide in German Politics after 1949), inside: Hans-Lukas Kieser and Dominik J. Schaller (Haz.) Der Völkermord an den Armeniern und die Shoah (Armenian Genocide and Shoah), (Zurich: 2002), p. 574, quoted by Gümüş Burak from footnote 46, Armenian Researches on Reasons for German Bundestag's Recognition of So-Called Armenian Genocide and Role of Political Protestantism, Ankara Winter 2005Autumn 2006, Issue: 20-21, p. 139

[16] Quoted by Gümüş Burak from Anette Schaefgen, age. p. 566-567, agm. p. 139

[17] Quoted by Gümüş Burak from Anette Schaefgen agm. p. 574, footnote 46.

[18] Quoted by Gümüş Burak from Anette Schaefgen, age. p. 566-567.

legislative and executive organ is far from being objective. It is also against their first resolution. Thus it is contrarian to principles of righteous expectation and stability.[19]

---

[19] Most realistic and stable attitude in this matter is adopted by England. When Armenian genocide allegations have been adopted in parliaments of Western countries one after another in later 1990's and early 2000's, England was also requested to adopt a similar resolution.

English State Minister Baroness Ramsey of Cartvale denied this request in the statement she made on behalf of British Government on 14 April 1999. "English Governments don't recognize the events happened in 1915 and 1916 as genocide as there is no document that proves the decision of Ottoman administration to exterminate Armenians. In our opinion it is not appropriate for today's governments to assess the events took place 80 years ago. Because these events are legal and historic arguments." http://www.publications.parliament.uk/pa/1d199899/ldhansrd/ vo990414/text/90414-09.htm.

In spite of this statement, the pressure of Armenian genocide lobby on England resulted in mentioning the Armenian genocide allegations during the Jewish Holocaust Commemoration to be held in London on 27 January 2001 but English Minister of Public Works and Environment, Beverly Hughes stated in the press conference she held in Ankara on 22 January 2001that only the Jewish Holocaust will be mentioned in commemoration (Milliyet, 2001) and she made the following statement to press in İstanbul on 24 January 2001.

"English Government went through the evidence submitted with regard to Armenian allegations a while ago. Reviewed documents related to events in 1915 and 1916. Decided that these events don't comply with the genocide description made by United Nations. This is English Government's attitude and shall not change." (Hürriyet, 2001).

Government Spokeswoman Baroness Scotland replied a question regarding this issue in writing on 7 February 2001 and said:

"Our government assessed in parallel with previous British governments that the events happened in Eastern Anatolia in 1915-1916 are not genocide as described in United Nations Genocide Convention dated 1948."

(http://www.un.org/documents/ga/ docs/55/a551008.pdf.) Gürkan, Uluç, Armenian Massacre Accusation, Judgement and Verdict (; Kaynak Publications, İstanbul, 2015, p.20-21

5. Assessment on Citing Germany's Own Experience in Resolution

In the decision of **European Court of Human Rights No. 27510/08** regarding **Perinçek/Switzerland case** it is clearly stated that; *"1915 events are different than Jewish holocaust"* and it is ensured that the two incidents cannot be compared.

On the other hand there are two major differences between these events: Jews didn't fight against Germany in 2nd World War but Armenians allied with enemies and fought against the Ottoman.

Therefore Germany's citing Jewish Holocaust in Parliament resolution is not to the point due to the explained reasons.

6. Assessment of Parliament Resolution in terms of Authority

The provision in **Article 25 of Constitution** states that; general principles of law of nations are an inseparable part of German Federal Law, they prevail the laws and they impose obligations along with directly binding rights for everybody living in German Federation.

It is also secured in **Article 20 of Constitution** that legislative acts cannot be contrary with constitutional order.

Convention on the Prevention and Punishment of the Crime of Genocide is internationally regarded as *"jus cogens"* (peremptory norm).

In Article 6 of Convention on the Prevention and Punishment of the Crime of Genocide it is stated that genocide could only be determined by a court decision and the law made by legislative organ without basing on an adjudication is null and void due to clear and obvious lack of jurisdiction.

As a matter of fact England and France, the occupation forces following the First World War took 144 Ottoman officers, bureaucrats and parliament members off to Malta and launched criminal proceedings about them between the dates of 3 January 1919 - 10 August 1921 **(2 years and 8 months)** in Ottoman State on the grounds that *"mistreating prisoners of war and massacring Armenians"* but in July 1921 the Crown Prosecution Office gave a verdict of non-prosecution on the grounds that ***"The evidence and information we have are insufficient to judge and punish the defendants in a criminal case".***

This verdict is very important because the events, witnesses and documents are obvious and this verdict had been given after the defeat of Ottoman. Anybody who respects law should not object this verdict.

European Court of Human Rights verdict dated 15 October 2015 No. 27510/08 in relation with **Perinçek/Switzerland case** concluded that only competent criminal court of the country where the event happened or **International Criminal Court** would render a verdict regarding the presence of a crime of genocide and within this context, judicial institutions other than competent criminal courts, parliaments, governments, academic institutions and even European Court of Human Rights cannot reach a verdict of genocide about the events in 1915 and forced migration cannot be deemed a genocide.

As the verdict of European Court of Human Rights binds the countries who are not parties to the legal proceedings, the resolution adopted constitutes a contradiction to decisions of European Court of Human Rights.[20]

In the case opened by an Armenian Association located in France with the allegation *"EU Candidate status of Turkey should be ceased as the European Parliament adopted a resolution stating 'Turkey carried out a genocide',"* **European Court of Justice** reached a verdict on 29 October 2004 and declared that *"The resolution adopted by European Parliament (EP) in 1987 with regard to Armenian Genocide is a political one and it has no validity in the field of law."*

Verdicts of European Court of Justice are binding with regard to EU member countries and therefore resolution of German Parliament is clearly a violation of EU Law.

French Constitutional Council (Court) cancelled the law drawn up by Patrick Deveciyan and adopted in French Parliament in 2006 which considers saying *"There is no Armenian genocide"* a crime.

The law titled ***"Recognition of 1915 Armenian Genocide No.2001/70"*** adopted and effectuated in 2001 was cancelled on 28 February 2012 by Constitutional Council's decision no. 647 due to the fact that two articles of the accepted law violate freedom of thought and expression, freedom of scientific research, freedom of communication and principle of legality of crime and punishment and principle of separation of powers and contradicts with Declaration of Rights of Man and the Citizen dated 1789 and French Constitution dated 1958.

---

[20] Justification of the decision on **Marckx v. Belgium case of European Court of Human Rights dated 13.06.1979 Application No. 6833/74**: *"As it is accepted, it is inevitable that the court decision would have effects going beyond the limits of this tangible case".*

Constitutional Council also decided on 8 January 2016 stated that in order to consider the act of denying a crime against humanity or denial of genocide a crime, the said crimes should have been confirmed by a decision of a competent court, that genocide is a fact based on a decision of an international court, but Armenian dissertation doesn't base on a court decision and legislative and executive organs don't have the authority to recognize an event as crime against humanity or genocide.

International Court of Justice (ICJ) adjudicated in a lawsuit brought by Croatia against Federal Republic of Yugoslavia in 1999 as follows: *"...forcing people who belongs to a group to emigrate from the place they live to another place cannot be regarded as genocide"*, *"...judgement of other countries by local courts in foreign countries is violation of international law"* and concluded that convention on genocide cannot have a retroactive effect.

The verdict of **European Court of Human Rights** dated 15 October 2015 and numbered **27510/08** with regard to **Perinçek/Switzerland case** it is stated that *"The forced emigration of Armenians in 1915 cannot be qualified as genocide pursuant to international law."*

Still accusing Turks in spite of these judicial decisions is disrespect to law to say the least.

International Court of Justice reached to a verdict on 3 February 2012 with regard to *"Jurisdictional Immunity of State, Germany-Italy: Greece is Intervener"* that judgement of countries by national court of another country doesn't carry a legal value and such a judgement violates international law[21].

7. Assessment of Resolution in terms of Jurisdiction, Right to a Fair Trial and Presumption of Innocence

Pursuant to **Article 11, Paragraph 1 of UN Declaration of Human Rights dated 1948,** a person who is accused in a penal offense is innocent pursuant to law without being legally judged open to the general public with regard to these allegations, pleaded and being found guilty.

Aforementioned resolution clearly violates the principle of "nobody would be deemed guilty without a court decision" pursuant to Universal Law. It also violates jurisdiction and right to a fair trial and prohibition to harm the essence of right specified in Article 19, Clause 2 of Constitution.

On the other hand members of parliament are only law-makers and it is strictly forbidden for them to use the authorization to act as a judge or a police in **Article 103, Clause 2 of German Constitution**. (**German Constitutional Court: BVerGE 47, 109 u.a.**) Therefore adjudication by members of parliament like a criminal judge is declared null and void.

8. Assessment of Resolution in terms of Inviolability of Human Dignity

With this resolution Turks have been humiliated and debased and their pride have been played with and thus, the

---

[21] http://www.icj-cij.org/docket/files/143/16899.pdf, 26.09.2014.

provision of inviolability of human dignity secured by **Article 1 of German Constitution** is violated.

9. Assessment of Resolution in terms of Expression

Turks were supressed with this resolution and their freedom of expression was limited by the state. Moreover, their opinion regarding non-occurrence of a genocide was tried to be altered by political pressure.

If the occurrence of genocide is mentioned in textbooks as a result of this resolution and if the students are asked about the date of genocide, explanations of genocides and which communities have committed the crime of genocide in exams, students will be forced to accept a genocide that they actually don't accept and reply these questions by saying Turks carried out a genocide in 1915 just for the sake of getting good marks. Thus the freedom of expression of students will be limited.

Due to the reasons explained above, this resolution clearly contradicts with the freedom of thought secured in **Article 5 of German Constitution.**

10. Assessment of Resolution in terms of UNESCO Criteria

Genocide will be included in textbooks due to the parliamentary resolution and this is contradicts with the principle and criterion stated in Article 20, Clause (g) of **Guidelines and Criteria for the Development, Evaluation and Revision of Curricula, Textbooks and Other Educational Materials in International Education**[22] published

---

[22] http://unesdoc.unesco.org/images/0010/001001/100178M.pdf (Access Date: 16.08.2016)

by UNESCO; *"...stereotypes and prejudices are avoided in the presentation of other cultures."*

11. Assessment of Resolution in terms of Other Articles of German Constitution and International Rules and Principles

Resolution is against the retrospectivity principle. **(German Constitution, Article 103, European Convention on Human Rights, Article 7)**

As the resolution brings Turkish and Armenian people face to face being void of legal basis and creates Turk and Islam animosity, it is against the objective of German People defined as *"to serve world peace"* in *"Preface"* of Constitution.

Assessment of German Federal Constitutional Court's Decision Dated 08.12.2016

1. Introduction

In the lawsuit filed in German Constitutional Court on 08.06.2016 on the basis of violation of our fundamental rights by the resolution of German Federal Parliament regarding the so-called Armenian Genocide dated 02.06.2016, **German Constitutional Court ordered a nonsuit on 08.12.2016** on the grounds that *"Plea of unconstitutionality is unacceptable. As the plaintiff (objector) did not sufficiently explain the possibility of violation of their fundamental rights and rights equal to fundamental rights and also such a possibility is not clear, this objection is void."*

Expression of "genocider" became a tool to humiliate Turks, especially in Europe. Due to the resolution of German Federal Parliament limiting expression of opinion regarding 1915 events and supressing both the plaintiff and all people primarily on freedom of thought and freedom of conscience ensured in **Article 9** and freedom of thought and other fundamental rights and freedoms such as freedom of thought and other fundamental rights and freedoms ensured in **Article**

10 of European Convention on Human Rights stated as *"1. Everybody has freedom of expression. This freedom includes freedom of opinion, freedom of information without interruption of public authorities and regardless of country borders,"* are severely and clearly restricted.

This restriction harms the plaintiff's rights and freedoms and constitutes a contradiction with fundamental principles of European Law. It also shakes **European and World Peace and Brotherhood** at their cores. Therefore dismissal of the lawsuit due to the lack of pre-conditions caused limitation of effective right to legal remedy which is the most important and discriminating characteristic of European civilization.

In this context the resolution contradicts with law and **development of democracy**.

2. Assessment of Resolution in terms of Obligation to Respect Human Rights

I am a citizen of the Republic of Turkey, the successor of claimant Ottoman Empire and not probing the lawsuit brought against my ancestors' being called genocider resulted in violation of obligation to respect human rights secured in Article 1 of European Court of Human Rights. There is no other accusing epithet more humiliating than calling a community, a society or nation "genocider". In case the German Federal Constitutional Court had been applied with by submitting only the above paragraph, it is clear that this application should have been investigated bur regardless of this fact, the verdict given in the contrary is clearly violates the **obligation to human rights** secured in **Article 1 of European Court of Human Rights.**

3. Assessment of Resolution in terms of Presumption of Innocence

On the other hand when it is considered that genocide is a crime, not examining the application against a criminal charge is contrary with the presumption of innocence defined in **Article 6/2 of European Convention of Human Rights** that *"Everyone charged with a criminal offence shall have the right to be presumed innocent until proved guilty according to the law."*
(**ECHR Salabaiku/France, 07/10/1988**)

4. Assessment of Resolution in terms of Right to a Fair Trial, Prohibition of Discrimination and Right to Legal Remedies

When the expression of *"...as there is no fact which is proved unmistakeably..."* about the so-called genocide in the decision of **European Court on Human Rights No: 27510/08** with regard to **Perinçek/Switzerland case** is considered, not implementing the law is a contrariety to Right to Fair Trial in **Article 6 of ECHR** and as genocide is not determined by a court order, and a also a contrariety to **Prohibition of Discrimination stated in Article 14 of ECHR** not giving the verdict from Armenians' point of view.

When it is considered that the plaintiff is a citizen of the Republic of Turkey, successor of Ottoman Empire, this resolution accusing our ancestors, citizens of the Republic of Turkey and the Turkish World with a very serious crime as a result of accepting the genocide had violated my fundamental rights and freedoms. The fact that the genocide resolution was adopted without a court decision against Ottoman Empire and not against Armenians proves that the resolution is against the principle of equality. Furthermore not determining Armenians who carried out genocide in both Ottoman Empire and Azerbaijan is also against equality.

Despite this, **right to legal remedies which is a part of right to fair trail** secured in **Article 6 of ECHR** is also violated by not investigating the allegations as to the accusations with regard to dispute.

5. Assessment of Resolution in terms of the Principle of Right to Access Court

The right to legal remedies is the prior condition of allowing people the right to be judged and of fair trial. The right to fair trial does not only involve opening a lawsuit but also guarantees this freedom in an opened case. (**ECHR Golder/England**, 21/02/1975), Resolution of German Federal Constitutional Court destroyed *"the right to access court"*. This universal assurance is clearly destroyed by state party, Germany.

Even though the said article of convention is a real, tangible and actually used assurance instead of providing theoretical and abstract freedom (**ECHR Hennigs/Germany, Philis/Greece)** this right is rejected by the German Federal Parliament by an injudicious and unsatisfactory justification.

6. Assessment of Resolution in terms of Right to Access Court and Right to Obtain Court Decision

In order for the right to remedy not to stay as an abstract right it is necessary to obtain *"a final judgement"* (**ECHR Marini/Albania**, Application No: 3738/02, 18/12/2007) but a verdict given by German Federal Constitutional Court which renders the right to access court meaningless/makes it nonfunctional/deactivates it (**ECHR** Application No: 2012/791, 7/11/2013) (**ECHR** Application No: 2013/500, 20/3/2014) and harming its essence (**ECHR Golder/United Kingdom,** Application No: 4451/70, 21/2/1975) annihilated the right to access court.

Furthermore they ignored the fact that instead of serving to provide rules of procedure, legal security and a fair judgement to manifest justice, becoming a kind of obstacle for the people to be judged by a competent court would violate the right to access court (**ECHR Efstathiou and Others/Greece**, Application No: 36998/02).

To sum up the resolution clearly violated the criteria of the right to access court's being a legitimate objective, being open and restrained and not creating a heavy burden on plaintiff (**ECHR** Application No: 2013/1613, 2/10/2013) and the criteria of not being as superior as preventing the access to court and not involving clear arbitrariness (**ECHR Maillard/France**, Application No: 35009/02, 6/12/2005).

On the other hand German Federal Parliament violated my right to obtain a decision from the court (Application No: 2013/500, 20/3/2014).

7. Assessment of Resolution in terms of Right to an Effective Remedy

German Federal Constitutional Court also blocked the right to an effective remedy and gave a verdict contradicting **Article 13 of ECHR** and by doing so, instead of blocking possible misuses, cleared the way for baseless resolutions to be taken by unauthorized administrative or politic units saying that the crime of genocide was. (**ECHR Karaçay/Turkey**, Application No: 6615/03, 27/03/2007, According to court; "*...not* *having an effective remedy would deprive the applicant of all kinds of assurances which would prevent misuse or provide auditing the similar corrections".)*

Trial of claimant actually means the trial of Turkish Nation. Thus the resolution caused **a narrow interpretation of right to legal remedies** and as this result is against the law, **it had a negative impact on development of European democracy.**

In this respect the resolution of German Federal Constitutional Court created multi-dimensional consequences as stated in **ECHR Marckx/Belgium,** Application No: 6833/74, 13/06/1979 decision; *"As it is accepted, it is inevitable that the court decision would have effects going beyond the limits of this tangible case".*

Right to Fair Trial is very important in a democratic community and interpreting this right narrowly cannot be regarded as legitimate (**ECHR Perez/France** Application No: 47287/99, 12/2/2004).

Therefore your esteemed court should protect the rights within the scope of individual application in such a manner that they would be *"applicable"* and *"efficient"* but not abstractly or theoretically. This principle is especially valid in terms of right to fair trial when its importance in a democratic society is considered. (**ECHR Stanev/ Bulgaria**, Application No: 36760/06, 17/1/2012).

8. **Assessment of Resolution in terms of Whether German Federal Constitutional Court is Seen as Independent or Not**

German Federal Constitutional Court gave a resolution which is contrary to the criterion of being seen as an independent institution (Application No: 2013/1134, 16/5/2013 and **Sramek/Austria, Benthem/Holland, Obermeier/Austria** and **İncal/Turkey** and **Çıraklar/ Turkey**).

Therefore the criterion of neutrally proving the authenticity of concern (**Çıraklar/Turkey**, Application No: 70/1997/854/1061, 28/10/1998 and **İbrahim Gürkan/Turkey,** Application No: 10987/10, 3/7/2012) is actualized in the incident.

In order to assure the neutrality and independency of German Federal Constitutional Court it is deliberately located in the capital, Berlin. In other words it is established in a city other than the old capital, Bonn and Munich, where the German Federal Intelligence Service (Bundesnachrichtendienst) is located. But due to the close relationship between the President of German Federal Constitutional Court and German mastermind, President of German Federal Constitutional Court is proposed to be President of Germany. This situation proves the relationship between German Federal Constitutional Court and German strategic mind and this is why they rejected the application without even investigating it as they are not neutral and independent in this sense.

9. Assessment of Resolution in terms of Right to Fair Trial

Therefore the right to air trial is clearly violated.

The application's not being rejected in a reasonable time shows that the court considered whether investigating the grounds or not and as it should be mandatory to accept the case if they investigate the grounds pursuant to **Article 6 of 1948 UN Convention on the Elimination of All Forms of Racial Discrimination,** they decided to reject the case without looking through it.

Not rejecting the case in a reasonable time resulted in violation of the right to fair trial.

When we consider that the case was rejected by German Federal Constitutional Court due to preconditions, the criterion of *"complexity of case"* (**ECHR İdalov/Russia**, Application No: 5826/03, 22/05/2012) and Turks' being named genociders and humiliated right after the resolution the criterion of "insecurity with respect to applicant within the scope of conflict" (**ECHR İdalov/Russia**, Application No: 5826/03, 22/05/2012) have been violated and the principle of being judged in a reasonable time is also violated.

Moreover even if these were missing (this doesn't mean acceptance) it is clear that time should have been granted to complete the said issues and materialize the violated rights but a contrariwise decision was given and this is clearly violation of right to fair trial.

10. Assessment of Resolution in terms of Right of Defence

Moreover even if these were missing (this doesn't mean acceptance) ECHR should have notified the opinion of the judge who reviewed the case to claimant and entitle the claimant to defence against this opinion. But they have submitted the file to Court Board in a way to result in conviction and result against us and caused the rejection of the file in terms of preliminary examination.

The report drawn up about the case was not notified to claimant (**ECHR Miran/Turkey**, Application No: 43980/04, 21/4/2009) and our right of reply to the report was inhibited. Moreover the file was argued about without holding a hearing and inviting the claimant. This is simply and clearly a violation of right to fair trial, principle of equality of arms and principle of adversarial proceedings.

11. Result

Decisions regarding determination of genocide are personal, social and political and not legal as it is explained.

Even though the decisions don't have legal characteristic, they are being made in order the genocide to be recognized by Turkey, to make Turkey grant land to Armenians and to constitute a base to pay compensation.

Even if it is very important to make statements by politicians against the genocide resolutions adopted by parliaments, to criticise the resolutions and to announce that they will be declared null and void opening cases against the resolutions is more important.

It should not be forgotten that the resolutions inhere the aim to prove the world that the Republic of Turkey was founded on genocide and therefore it is not a legitimate state along with forcing recognition, land grant and compensation.

Epilogue

In our study the genocide resolution of German Federal Parliament and the decision accepted by German Federal Constitutional Court with regard to this resolution are assessed only from the point ow law.

We especially tried to reveal within the frame of documents and information that the resolution of Parliament doesn't have a legal basis, is against equality and condemns Turks with an ex parte perspective.

As will be understood from our study, we tried to explain that accepting the decision of Constitutional Court cannot be possible in the light of leading cases of ECHR.

Rejection of the case by Constitutional Court without assessing the grounds proved the rightfulness of our arguments and the fact that the German Federal Constitutional Court actually doesn't have any argument to legitimize the Parliament.

Wishing the rule of law to hold sway the whole world and not experience new *"legal scandals"*.

Bibliography

1. German Federal Republic Constitution. 1949

2. Anonymous, 1990, 'Armenian Declaration of Independence', http://www.gov.am/en/independence/ 2010-08-01, access: 30/ 07 / 2016.

3. Anette Schaefgen, Der Vörlkmord an den Armeniern in der deutschen Politik nach 1949 (Armenian Genocide in German Politics after 1949), inside: Hans-Lukas Kieser and Dominik J. Schaller: HansLukas Kieser ve Dominik J. Schaller (Haz.) Der Völkermord an den Armeniern und die Shoah (Armenian Genocide and Shoah), (Zurich: 2002), p. 574, quoted by Gümüş Burak from footnote 46, Armenian Researches on Reasons for German Bundestag's Recognition of So-Called Armenian Genocide and Role of Political Protestantism, Ankara Winter 2005-Autumn 2006, Issue: 20-21, p. 139

4. ECHR GRAND CHAMBER. Perinçek/Switzerland case decision," 27510/08". 15/12/2015

5. ECHR. Marckx/Belgium Case Decision,"6833/74 ". 13/06/1979

6. Armenia throughout the history, http://www. Armenica.org; Access: 5 June 2014

7. Constitution of the Republic of Armenia,1995.

8. Armenian Massacre Accusation, Judgement and Verdict (Kaynak Publications, İstanbul, 2015, p.20-21

9. Historical Map of Armenia
    http://www.armeniaforeignministry.com, Access: 5 June 2014

10. http://www.un.org, access: 30/ 07/ 2016.

11. Lütem, Ö. Ergin,2010," *Returning to Zero Point in Protocols"*,
    http://www.avim.org.tr/degerlendirmetekli.
    php?makaleid=322,25/07/2016. 25/07/2016

12. International Court of Justice, Jurisdictional Immunity of State, Germany-Italy: Greece is Intervener Decision 2012/2.   03/02/2016,
    http://www.icjcij.org/docket/files/143/16899.pdf,
    access:25/07/2016